QUESTIONS
IN THE
VESTIBULE

QUESTIONS IN THE VESTIBULE

Poems

RACHEL HADAS

TriQuarterly Books/Northwestern University Press

Evanston, Illinois

TriQuarterly Books
Northwestern University Press
www.nupress.northwestern.edu

Copyright © 2016 by TriQuarterly Books/Northwestern University Press. Published 2016 by TriQuarterly Books/Northwestern University Press. All rights reserved.

Printed in the United States of America

10 9 8 7 6 5 4 3 2 1

Library of Congress Cataloging-in-Publication Data
Names: Hadas, Rachel
Title: Questions in the vestibule : poems / Rachel Hadas.
Description: Evanston, Illinois : TriQuarterly Books/Northwestern University Press, 2016.
Identifiers: LCCN 2015041074| ISBN 9780810133174 (pbk. : alk. paper) | ISBN 9780810133181 (e-book)
Classification: LCC PS3558.A3116 Q47 2016 | DDC 811.54—dc23 LC record available at http://lccn.loc.gov/2015041074

The paper used in this publication meets the minimum requirements of the American National Standard for Information Sciences—Permanence of Paper for Printed Library Materials, ANSI Z39.48–1992.

For Shalom

CONTENTS

Acknowledgments   *xi*

ONE

Threshold   *5*
Nest   *6*
Messengers   *7*
Mandala in Mirror   *8*
Reading in the Garden   *10*
Three Bedrooms   *12*
The Second Floor   *13*
My Mother's Smile   *15*
The Yawn   *16*
The Thread   *17*
Arm in Arm   *18*
To Reconcile the Raspberries   *19*
Hugger-Mugger Road   *20*
On the Beach   *21*
Six Summer Days and Nights   *22*
Oubliette   *23*
Quest   *24*
Sleepover   *25*
Wind Songs   *26*
The Blue Changes   *27*

TWO

Afternoon in Between   *31*
Courtyard   *32*

Hindsight   33
Glimpses   34
The Veil and the Baby   35
Dreams and Stories   36
Ghost Yogurt   37
In the Kitchen   38
Feast   39
The Ever After   40
After Long Sleep   41
Questions in the Vestibule   43
Red Chair   44
Empty Studio, National Arts Club   45
White Petals   47
Van   48
Riding Backward   49
On the Bank   50
Stepping Stones   51
Hurry, Red Fruit, Descent   57
In the Theater   60

THREE

Covered Basket   63
The Break   66
Valentine's Day   69
Full and Empty Room   70
Balancing   71
Cento   72
Aubade   74
Green and Gold   75
The Lost Bottle   77
Roosevelt Hospital Blues   79
Sailing in the Sky   82

Syrup and a Waffle   83

Sunroof Test-Drive Ice Storm   85

After Independence Day   86

Still Lives   87

Two Lakes   89

Elemental: Offering to Yemaya   91

Lying in Wait   93

Bliss   94

Equipoise   96

Slow Green   97

Parents   98

But It's True   99

Daffodil Notebook   101

Poetreef   104

ACKNOWLEDGMENTS

Grateful acknowledgment is made to the following publications in which
these poems appeared, sometimes in different forms or with different titles:

Alhambra Poetry Calendar, "Still Lives"
American Arts Quarterly, "Empty Studio, National Arts Club"
Angle, "After Long Sleep," "Hurry, Red Fruit, Descent"
Bellevue Literary Review, "In the Theater," "The Second Floor"
The Book of Scented Things, "The Lost Bottle"
The Chronicle Review, "Hugger-Mugger Road," "On the Beach,"
    "To Reconcile the Raspberries"
The Common Review, "The Ever After"
First Things, "Balancing," "Equipoise," "Slow Green," "Wind Songs"
The Hopkins Review, "After Independence Day," "The Break"
The Hudson Review, "Mandala in Mirror," "Oubliette"
The New Criterion, "Quest," "Questions in the Vestibule," "White Petals"
New Republic, "Aubade"
The New Yorker, "The Yawn"
The Paris Review, "The Veil and the Baby"
Per Contra, "Nest"
phati'tude Literary Magazine, "Feast"
Poetry, "Green and Gold," "Sleepover"
Poets.org, "Messengers"
Pulse, "Lying in Wait"
Raritan, "Afternoon in Between," "Six Summer Days and Nights"
The Saint Ann's Review, "Reading in the Garden"
The Times Literary Supplement, "Poetreef," "Roosevelt Hospital Blues"
Upstreet, "Sailing in the Sky"
Virginia Quarterly Review, "The Blue Changes," "Red Chair"
The Yale Review, "Ghost Yogurt"

QUESTIONS
IN THE
VESTIBULE

ONE

THRESHOLD

The in-between is queasy,
but all is in between.

Midsummer green? Monotonous
when everything is green.

The sea? A glittering question
if everything is sea.

This vestibule? Unsettling.
I teeter first one way

and then the other. In
or out? I am a fool

to be so caught off balance.
All is vestibule.

NEST

Lying in bed,
I walk the road
inside my head.
All but impossible
not to follow
hand over hand
the quaking bridge,
the snaking rope;
not put together
thought by thought
twig by twig
strand chip thread
button by bead by domino,
not weave and twist
a world in progress
between my fingers,
and not to complete
a nest in which
to curl and shift
and wait for what
may come, may come
over the threshold
of one more dawn.

MESSENGERS

draw near at dawn and then recede
even if you beckon them.
They loom like demons
you tug by the tail to examine from up close
and then let fly away.
Their colors at once brighter and less bright
than you remembered, they
hover and insinuate all day
at the corner of your eye.

MANDALA IN MIRROR

I'm sunning myself on a bench
in the center strip of Broadway.

A youth I recognize—
I used to know his mother—

strides across the street,
carrying a tall mirror.

I'm thinking of mandalas,
and as I start to chant this to myself,

out comes *Young man carrying mandala*,
which, wheel-like, turns: mandala

carrying mirror, mandala
mirroring the scene,

mirroring an old man
(bearded, with straw hat)

crossing the same street,
mirroring me here,

soaking in the sunny afternoon.
Mandala as porthole

through which one sees below
the surface of the ocean;

as dome of an arched ceiling
that opens to the sky;

or differently again,
cross-section of the brain,

mandala/MRI.
All this the mirror carries,

tucked under the boy's arm.
From underneath his other

arm a skateboard juts.
The beautiful and young

sense that the old observe them
and do not know or care

when we look at them
what it is we see.

READING IN THE GARDEN

In the garden of the Hotel Ganesh Himal,
epic shrinks to lyric with a plot.

I pause at a passage I don't remember
having read before, although I must have.

Set in hell and drawing on Greek myth,
the vignette's fiercely human.

The fallen angels shuttle back and forth
incessantly. What is it they are seeking?

They ferry over this Lethean Sound
Both to and fro, their sorrow to augment,

And wish and struggle, as they pass, to reach
The tempting stream, with one small drop to lose

In sweet forgetfulness all pain and woe,
All in one moment, and so near the brink.

That last word rhymes with the verb thirsty
fallen angels can't achieve. Oblivion,

in hell's eternity so tantalizing,
terrifies us while we walk the earth.

Accordingly I write the passage down
and read it back into the afternoon

against the quiet bubbling of a fountain
while this walled garden shuts the city out.

THREE BEDROOMS

Heart of the house, connubial olive tree
carved into the marriage bed from which
to enter every morning's fresh familiar world.
Those years away gave the wandering hero
the impetus to reach his goal.
He reached it; whereupon
the room seemed smaller, shabbier than before.
Having arrived, he itched to leave again.

I try to visit in the afternoon,
when I am tired, and to stretch out beside him.
Yesterday I lay down
and fell asleep and dreamed
that both of us were in our bed at home,
and woke into the strangeness of his room.

THE SECOND FLOOR

for Amy Pizzella

You said that in your dream you couldn't find
your father, Sam, he had diminished so.
You raced, a harried pilgrim to a shrine,

up and down corridors and to and fro.
Or not a place of worship but a station:
announcements, crowds, anxiety, but no

familiar face or any information.
Wait: a Sam-like figure seemed to scoot
ahead of you to some dark destination.

The folding doors swung open and then shut.
As quickly on their short legs toddlers move,
tall parents lumbering in slow pursuit,

so they speed onward, people whom we love—
first close, but soon more distant; finally some
out of reach well before the grave

hides them. At most we're granted a last dim
glimpse in some realm of indeterminacy.
One afternoon I peeked into Sam's room.

He lay, his body folded in a Z,
so frail that he seemed poised to disappear,
float from the bed and lightly slip away

from the second floor into the air.
Before I left the second floor for good
that day, I peeked again. Now you were there

too: daughter, father cradled on the bed
in one kind curve, at rest, your four eyes shut.
Sleep and love, the quick, the nearly dead:

back I tiptoed from that double gate.
I never saw Sam—not in life—again.
His final passage took some weeks to set,

and I was traveling. While I was gone,
you emailed me your dream of flight and loss.
Or was it a shared dream? Or only mine?

All possible. I too was giving chase
to a phantom, fugitive and fading—
a husband, not a father, in my case,

roaming the floor and silently receding.

MY MOTHER'S SMILE

Her hair still hardly touched with gray, and wound
in gleaming braids around her head, my mother,
who in life was not so given to smiling,
grinned in last night's dream from ear to ear
the double meaning of archaic smiles:
"I am alive" and also "I am dead."

A snapshot from the fifties, black and white:
there stands my mother, sturdy, tan, and beaming,
each arm around a daughter. And all three
are squinting in the same morning sun
that lit that joyful smile that lit the dream.

THE YAWN

My visiting tall son
is sleepy. His sweet gape
brings back his father's yawn.
Seeing our lost husband and lost father
suddenly conjured up, I laugh. My son
frowns. Does he think
it's at him I'm laughing?
The cat opens her mouth to mew.
The orphaned piano: it yawns too.

THE THREAD

"Sit still," said Wendy, mending Peter's shadow,
sewing the strayed creature
back onto its restless owner.

What ties me to my life?
Sewn to the world by love and habit, how
to loosen stitches but not cut the thread?

Can a whole seam
ease, breathe, give
and still not come undone?

ARM IN ARM

Light was beginning to gild the attic room
where I'd been sleeping in a single bed.
Plausible visitations at dawn,
bending so deftly into opening day
that they feel much more like memory.

This was what I remembered: he and I
were walking arm in arm
and talking. We agreed to start afresh,
repair the damage. Moving: a new chance.
It would be possible, it would be simple.
The way stretched clear before us.
The illness shrank into a silly spat,
nothing unfixable, already small
behind us as we walked into the future.

TO RECONCILE THE RASPBERRIES

Where this path goes I know.
How long, and winding how, there is no telling.
No turning back. The pace is very slow.

Whose path I don't remember: his or mine?
Can I step off to the side,
let him trudge on alone?

Can I say in tomorrow morning's light
one more time, "It's over,"
the latest misdemeanor from last night?

The track is rough. I teeter to and fro.
And steep. Again the questions, again:
Does he recognize you?

Heat lightning, crescent moon,
ripe raspberries. How to reconcile
these with the brutal road?

Here is the hammock slung in its old place
between the same two trees.
But how to conjure up the dream of rest?

The hammock in my mind
I can lie down in, I can sway and read.
The raspberries hang. Not a breath of wind.

HUGGER-MUGGER ROAD

He walked into her room (she was in bed)
and tried to drape a blanket over her head.

"That's the last straw!" the director cried.
No: one more step on Hugger-Mugger Road,

not first, not last. I follow in his wake.
He strides, then slows. The final goal will take

how long to reach? Oh do not estimate.
So zigzag is the path that its few straight

stretches seem deceptive. Then stand still.
The road is winding, but it's all downhill.

What's the hurry? This is not a race.
Sometimes I sense sunlight on my face

and rest a little, shift the heavy load
as he and I proceed down Hugger-Mugger Road.

ON THE BEACH

Our son and I are bouncing up and down
in shallow surf and batting back and forth
the only topic all this gold and azure
boils down to, the old question
to which there is no answer, though we toss
the ball of speculation to and fro.
Here he is now—how could I not have seen him?

Tall sea creature, unspeaking,
smiling a little, bouncing in the waves
along with us, leaping and lithe, his silence
lost in the splash and spray
as the shriek of a child is covered by a gull's cry.
Parallel to the horizon, this strip of sand
has no beginning and no end.

SIX SUMMER DAYS AND NIGHTS

Friday afternoon I give away
three of my husband's much-washed flannel nightshirts
to my son, his girlfriend, and another friend.
They put them on like a cult uniform
over their jeans and go to light a bonfire
of dank old wood extracted from the barn.
Sometime Saturday
an overloaded bough,
weighed down by early apples, cracks and breaks.
Baskets of apples need to be picked up.
Monday: the widowed neighbor's dog's strong tail
bruises my leg. Tuesday: "People on
this planet," says our angry neighbor, "have
five more years to go." And Wednesday night
the full moon layers its glow
deep in the night over the fields like snow.

One old bough broken by its fragrant load.
One ranting neighbor with his long black beard.
One leaping dog. One bruise. One gleaming moon.
Three widows on the road, of whom I am
and also am not one.
An absence walking in my husband's shape.
The presence of my son.

OUBLIETTE

Numberless, the ways
of shaping what is not:
in breaths that rise like smoke
and wreathe and curl and spread
or plummet straight as lead
propelled by its own weight.
Small enough to fit into a fist,
the heavy ones drop straight
into an oubliette
black and echoless.
What goes up vanishes,
also what comes down.
Nothing is permanent.
Everything is.

QUEST

Scrambling down gullies, fording icy streams,
staggering over snow crust that keeps breaking

so I keep sinking in up to my thighs,
then pulling out a sodden leg again,

first one leg, then the other, barely moving
forward, pursued, pursuing, which is which,

I stumble to a hut at the edge of the forest
where a band of merciful young outlaws

shelter me, give me dry boots, a blanket,
feed me, let me rest awhile by their fire.

I mustn't sleep. I must be on my way.
The darkness is unyielding, and the cold.

Tangle of black branches. Lantern light on snow.
A friendly little square of firelit window

behind me, but again I am pursued,
pursuing: quest, flight, exile. Dawn. Pale sky.

Black boulders line the road. Between steep banks
a brackish stream is trickling downhill.

SLEEPOVER

Ida and Isidor Straus sleep side by side
eternally in an Egyptian galley
fronting their Woodlawn mausoleum.
Symbolically lie. Their boat is small;
nor was her body recovered from the *Titanic*.
And yet the image of the voyage holds.

Why not embark? A river runs behind me
on the other side of this dark window.
A dream called Night Boat
arranged us side by side in a black craft,
sailing the river of forgetfulness
until the stars went out.

It was poetic license. I didn't dream that boat.
The boat was dream, and we were passengers
balanced on the slippery cusp of daylight,
unless he had already disembarked
in some shadowy port,
leaving me to sail along alone.

WIND SONGS

i

A great wind blew over us.
Some of us stared into it with streaming eyes;
some of us muffled our heads in scarves;
some of us hid our faces in our hands.
After the gust we looked at one another.
It took some time to understand the change:
the ground was shifting underneath our feet.

ii

I would have liked to linger by the fire
but a rough wind was blowing.

To wake up and go back to sleep
but pale dawn was showing.

Down on the river, a boat with a black sail.
I must be going.

THE BLUE CHANGES

Channel, brook, stream—call it a river
that flows past the hospital
in different shades and seasons of blue
glittering harmlessly in noonday sun.
Then a sudden change.
Yesterday he was alive. Today he's dead.

He seems to be more alive now that he's dead:
a continuous transition, one flowing river
twisting and turning, meandering through change.
Some days we gazed out at it from the hospital
solarium, basking sleepily in the sun.
Right up until the end I took that blue

gaze for granted. One day: no more blue,
not where that came from. Once a person is dead,
they no longer see the light of the sun.
He's standing on the far bank of the river.
Tiny as a dollhouse now, the hospital
is no longer home. I turn to face the change.

There is no way to anticipate the change
flooding from anger red to twilight blue.
One August afternoon in the hospital
from the room across the hall they wheeled a dead
person. That day the photogenic river
was a regatta: sailboats, sparkling sun.

Mysterious adjustments out of the sight of the sun:
the current flowing toward the harbor changes
its mind. A black ship's anchored in the river.

Night-sky blue or light-sky blue:
which is the proper hue to drape the dead?
The city has become one hospital,

and not the healing kind of hospital
but a place of transformation. Father, son,
mother—whole families emerge, not dead
exactly, but bewildered by the change.
All winter you can hear the sharp wind blow.
Then rain and snowmelt thaw the frozen river.

The hospital has vanished. He is dead.
I look up: blue sky. Sun.
Turn backward in your courses, sacred rivers.

TWO

AFTERNOON IN BETWEEN

You came to meet me in the in-between.
I rose to greet you in the empty room.
The house was silent, absent. Afternoon
had superseded morning, clouds and rain
blurring the early promise of the sun.
Light wasn't fading yet. It wasn't warm,
but neither was it cool enough to need
a fire. I padded through the chilly house.
Projects and processes not yet quite done
or long ago abandoned filled the space.
This all was preparation for departure.
I tried to wave good-bye; reflections
watched me in the window.
I rose on tiptoe but saw no one,

so sat down on the floor,
cross-legged on the hearthrug, near a fire
I had lit after all, and took a break
into deeper stillness—so I thought.
A door had opened. I could hear the creak.
Footsteps on the stair? There was a crack.
Who was approaching—not from where, from when?
I strained to hear in the still-ringing room.
Lost but not forgotten, oh come back.
All-purpose jacket for the changing weather,
liminality is what we wear.
I rose to greet you in the arc of air.
I reached my hand out. Were you waiting there?
Let's move through the in-between together.

COURTYARD

Open the windows. Empty the drawers
of years of old nail clippings.
In the courtyard, decades of dead leaves.
Clear away the clutter and the rubble.
Sift and sift until the wind has dropped.
Only once the background is swept clean
can a fresh foreground slide into place.
That stretch of emptiness—call it the future.
There is no end to the spaciousness of sky.

The courtyard gleams. You pause on your way in
or out to admire the vista.
No wind. You can take off the fur-lined cloak,
whose thick folds now feel smothering and hot.
A new wind is rising,
but not a wind for which you'll need a wrap.
There is no end to the spaciousness of sky.

HINDSIGHT

The black pup frisked ahead,
splashing through puddles; joyful, doubled back,
eyes gleaming, tongue lolling out.
So long as she'd been trotting close behind me,
dogging my heels, I hadn't seen her. Now
I wondered how I could have been so blind;
rolled out of bed, opened the curtains. Snow
blanketed the landscape, and the sky
seemed unable to make up its mind
which end this was of the brief winter day.
Where was my dog? I didn't understand.
Intuition hidden in plain sight:
a figure in the threshold, gift in hand,
stood there and didn't say.

GLIMPSES

The cat, not eating, lighter day by day.
Glossy whale backs surface and slide under.
A hole his shape, a shadow in the air.
Jostling dreams breach and sound again.
Whale words are too deep for us to hear.
The dying cat spoke with her whole small life.

Through the last years he drifted silently.
Absent, present, he's still hard to see.
As if we ever garner more than glimpses:
tail and fin, even if seen again,
are somewhere else and never quite the same.
The whales converse inaudibly below.

THE VEIL AND THE BABY

The veil between the worlds is growing thin.
The grass is growing tall outside the door.
Who was that baby in the dream again?

Time to re-re-read Colin McGinn
on moral literacy. Less is more.
The veil between the worlds is growing thin.

Sailing out of sight: the Circle Line,
painted golden in the sunset's glare.
Who was that baby in the dream? Again

I cast about for answers and find none.
The country: over here. The city: there.
The veil between the two is wearing thin.

Poetry: a game of telephone,
each changing place with that which goes before.
Whose baby was that in the dream again?

Youth, beauty passed me riding on the train.
The final threshold is interior.
The veil between the worlds is tough but thin.
The baby in the dream appears again.

DREAMS AND STORIES

Dreams: understood but not remembered.
In this they are the opposite of stories,
even though stories are composed of dream stuff,
and when we tell our dreams we have to use
shreds and threads drawn from the web of story.

Dreams: remembered but not understood.
In this they are the opposite of stories,
even though dreams are mostly told in the guise of stories,
and when we tell a story we are nailing
narrative scaffolding to the stuff of dreams.

Sleep's book holds more than we can ever read.
We stick a finger in the text,
pull out a plum and lick it.
Later, in the middle of the morning,
a ghost taste floats back.

GHOST YOGURT

Line a deep bowl with cheesecloth—or in my
kitchen, with a pillowcase worn thin,
    threadbare as gauze. Dump in
a quart or so of yogurt. Let it strain.
    As the whey
drips through the sheer fabric, let it pool
    in the bowl awhile
and then discard. What yogurt will remain
is denser, more acerbic, almost dry.
    Less is more: a mere
spoonful of it now goes a long way.
    And we?
Are years the cheesecloth, so we drip and drain,
ourselves the milky residue we toss?
    Or is it time
that hour by day by year is strained through us,
steadily reduced to more itself,
stronger, purer, more distilled from less?
The either and the or: they both are true.
    We fall through time; it passes through
    us. Therefore
    both are less, both more,
nourished by refuse, by what we refuse,
    enriched by waste and loss.
The survivor is victorious.

IN THE KITCHEN

Heads together at the kitchen table,
you and I slice and dice ingredients
we each have brought, the fruits of two long harvests,
taken apart and then put back together.
We drop them in the pot and stir the brew

counterclockwise. Breathing in the steam
of one another's stories, we construe:
part intuition, part improvisation,
wholly reciprocal. This broth of dream
we now proceed to thicken, tossing in

as binders memories, visions, and delusions.
What else is subtle, thick,
and also has a binding? Why, a book.
Shut your eyes. Open the book at random.
Put a finger down on the blind page.

Open your eyes and look.
Where have you landed in the mystic tome?
Open the window and let in some air.
The cauldron cools. Dream soup:
strong medicine. The story's almost done.

FEAST

A feast whose preparation has claimed years
ravenous feeders speedily consume.
Heaped platters scoured bare;
a burnt crust here, a gnawed rind there,
a shell sucked dry, a bone.
Sensing they've reached the end of appetite,
do avid revelers ever pause midbite,
or does no surfeit fill the gaping maw?
The law says Vanish. We obey the law.

THE EVER AFTER

I swung in a swing and listened to a fable
read by my host in a voice that sometimes broke.

His son's train sets colonized the floor.
His family was elsewhere, as was mine.

Or did I have a family? That year
we each inhabited our lives alone.

This sounds like allegory, but it's true.
If we are lucky, this is what we do:

stop and listen, swinging to and fro,
to old stories a fresh voice makes new.

The fable's moral? We weren't of one mind.
But we agreed about the ever after.

AFTER LONG SLEEP

Have you ever slept so long that when
you woke you were all groggy, time and space
in need of disentangling? And then,
having gotten up and washed your face,
were no less baffled, still at a loss?
Though now this was a scene you recognized—
you could name the city, street, and house—
something salient remained disguised
or missing; yes, some treasure that you prized.
A mirror beckoned and you acquiesced.
No nightmare; you took stock and realized
this was yourself, beauty and youth effaced.
Break the mirror. Turn and face the sky;
walk toward water. So it was with me.

And pronouns having slipped off like a skin,
found a beach and stood there, feet in cold
salt water, and allowed it to sink in:
that years had passed. I ("I") had gotten old.
That there was still a future to unfold
somewhere up ahead, unknown duration,
another story waiting to be told.
Into the sea I tossed my lamentation
and fished out something different: exultation,
survival—unfamiliar, dripping wet,
and eager with a wholly new narration
innocent of fear and of regret.
Let gory vampires gnash their fangs with thirst.
The scars were scarred. Bad dreams had done their worst.

Hair and skin now glimmering and white,
was there some secret sill that I had crossed?
In-between sky: a crescent moon still bright,
a pink horizon to the west or east.
Does what awaits us balance what we've lost?
Interior queries call for no response.
Not every question needed to be voiced.
The moon had set. I didn't speak for once.
This late-earned patience shading into trance
silently spread against the changing sky,
balanced between before and after, dance
performed by everyone until we die.
And after? It was early. It was late.
There was no one to interrogate.

A vague emergency from long ago:
rumblings and clashes as of war.
My dreams are rarely interrupted now
by rumors from the City of Before,
where I camped out a dozen years or more.
How the chaos faded, when or why
I left the region, I no longer care.
I am outdoors. I'm gazing at the sky,
a sloping meadow; cattle graze nearby.
Could this placid pastoral be mine?
Something tells me that I cannot stay
here in the paradise of in-between.
Beyond the hill's curve, a blue glint. A sea?
An interlude. A possibility.

QUESTIONS IN THE VESTIBULE

Ready to take the first decisive step,
you pull your purpose round you like a cloak.
A draft stirs, chilly, stale,
redolent of some half-remembered mix:
anticipation, appetite, regret.
If the liminal can be called a place,
this place might bear your name,
if you have a name, who hesitate
to step over the threshold.
Successive selves superimposed
form a Muybridge composite, frenetic,
blurry, yet motionless,
body suspended in its bustling progress,
each movement slivered as it arcs through space.
Zeno's paradox: how many baby
steps will take you through that door? Divide
each gesture or each inch in two: the process
slows to a crawl. Is it a one-way passage,
and if so, which way were you heading?
Will simply standing still defer time's flow?
The dust motes swirl, and there you are, abstracted
in the chamber of the in-between
where if there were a window you might see
seasons, a bare tree, a setting moon.
At first you think that you'll be moving on.

RED CHAIR

In flight: bird, arrow.
Static: a red chair
waiting for someone in a patch of sun
that when you turn to look again is gone.
Blue jays bouncing. Early afternoon.
Urgent message of that dream at dawn
whose theme was stripping, scouring: clean, clean,

but evanescent as a breath upon
a freezing pane. So clear a space and see
in the wintry gold of three o'clock
just as shadows start to lengthen
the chair gone suddenly vermilion.
Leaf by leaf the trees turn bare.
And now a blue jay tries the empty chair.

EMPTY STUDIO, NATIONAL ARTS CLUB

I sit and look out the window
north over Gramercy Park,
licking the salt of Indian summer
off my upper lip.

Yellows are passing in the street:
a manila folder; a blouse;
a slicker. What did we do to deserve
brilliance such as this,

caught between hot summer
and fall's aridity,
a dry and thirsty season
for the city and for me?

Anyway, thank you, yellow!
I toast you with a glass
of warm white wine abandoned
on the carved mantelpiece

of this ornate studio.
For hours—more likely days—
no one has ventured into this room
to look out over the trees

that canopy Gramercy Park. By now
from high summer's rich green,
the leaves have begun to thicken
and dry like cheese or wine.

Since Samuel Tilden built this house
a century ago and more,
someone has slapped a tobacco-brown
rug on the inlaid floor.

One of the windows has been plugged up.
An air conditioner wheezes
and rattles to discourage
October's sultry breezes.

Spindly-legged plastic chairs
piled in a crooked heap
resemble oversized locusts
waiting to take a leap.

Missing none or all of this,
ironic, reticent,
a wall-sized mirror renders back
the room at a dusky slant,

allowing my abstractions
to drift on its vast glaze.
Chewy husks of protein—
bodies of drowned fruit flies—

float in my glass. Yet since it savors
of this still afternoon,
right up as far as my closed lips
I tilt the acrid wine.

WHITE PETALS

White petals suddenly strewing the sidewalk
smell yeasty, salty, faintly edible.

They have appeared from nowhere all at once.
Not only because of the mild weather,

this past winter felt to me like fall.
So this season, softly swallowed up

into not spring but summer,
offers more of the same confusion.

One thing is clear, or clearer: your long fading,
so slow to live for both of us, is over.

That endless-seeming zone is now as distant
as if I had ventured down a crooked staircase

into a rancid restaurant in a dim cellar
and quickly up and out again—there was nothing for me there.

Finding my way home through unfamiliar streets,
I heard a bird hidden in the new foliage.

Clouds floated overhead.
The sidewalk was spotted with white petals.

VAN

Packed with young people munching sandwiches
(the sandwich maker's busy on the roof),

a van is careening down a snowy road
along whose slippery shoulder I am walking.

It drives right past me but immediately turns back.
They had forgotten to pick me up and then remembered.

I am relieved to be given a ride
to wherever we are going.

Complicated sleeping arrangements fade
into the genial muddle of the night.

Transportation. Voices. Sleep. Food. Snow.
No plot. Nothing happened.

Yet morning shimmers with a hopeful halo.
Grasses that grow in water sway with a current

that touches and transforms them and flows on.
It will flow on without me. But the morning:

shining pebbles, hardy winter weeds
gleaming in patches where the snow has melted;

the jolting van packed with young passengers;
the sandwich maker laughing on the roof.

RIDING BACKWARD

Where snow gives light back, thus prolonging day,
and road and river run
now perpendicular, now parallel
to the tracks, and north is the direction
(as it was every summer's destination)
is my way. January afternoon:
this seat's not in the designated Quiet
Car, but all the same no one is talking
as we're borne facing backward toward the past
or future. Vertical and horizontal:
stark trees, strung wires, plowed road, white field, black river
patchily frozen, though if I knelt down
I think my lips could touch the mother water.

ON THE BANK

Ending, beginning, aging, feeling young,
knowing less and more,
you're standing on a riverbank
keeping your balance on the slippery stones.
Having learned over decades to hold still,
you stand there, watch the flow,
observe the currents swaying to and fro,
and suddenly lose your footing and slide into the turbid water.

It's automatic, even cold and wet,
to surface, shake the water from your hair,
recite a list of all the things you think
you no longer need. But not so fast.
A narrative has already
begun to spin a web
anchored to a twig
jutting out over the hungry water.
Both web and twig appear so fragile
you hardly dare to look
for fear that one or both of them will break.

STEPPING STONES

A column made of light,
visible from afar,
a beacon in the night.
A column made of light:
isolated, straight,
not close to any shore.
A column made of light,
visible from afar.

A single candle glows,
cupped between two hands;
its radiance barely shows.
A single candle glows,
clasped by one who knows.
No one else understands.
A single candle glows,
cupped between two hands.

Step over the sill
and cross from here to there.
Threshold invisible:
step over the sill
uncertainly. This goal
is all interior.
Step over the sill
and cross from here to there.

Trust in the hands that take
and lay you in the deep
blue bath of stars, awake.

Trust in the hands that take
you, opening the book
of dreams. You're not asleep.
Trust in the hands that take
and lay you in the deep.

Ashes in a cloud
are drifting down the stream.
Do not turn your head.
Ashes in a cloud
you yourself have spread
change from grit to foam.
Ashes in a cloud
are drifting down the stream.

Expanse of ocean—water
as far as I can see.
Mother, am I your daughter?
Expanse of ocean water
glimmering green and gray,
the waves' unnumbered laughter.
Expanse of ocean—water
as far as I can see.

A beacon shines alone.
Shelter your flame, then step
over a sill. Lie down.
The beacon shines alone.
The ash cloud borne along
the brook: where will it stop?
Your beacon shines. Alone,
shelter your flame. Then step.

White gate, red bird, new day:
the after and before
ambiguously at play.

Red bird, new gate, white day
show simultaneously
vistas of less and more.
Red gate, white bird, new day.
The after and before.

The thing about one's past
is how it fades away
like that into the mist.
The thing about a past
is that, though it looks vast,
it fits inside one day.
The thing about the past
is how it fades away.

Your suitcase, bulging, black;
my overnight bag small.
I never learned to pack.
Your suitcase, bulging, black:
would you be coming back?
Had I been here at all?
Your suitcase, bulging, black;
my overnight bag small.

Remembered colonnade
out of de Chirico:
blue-black stillness. Dread.
Remembered colonnade.
Chatting with the dead,
the living amble through.
Remembered colonnade
out of de Chirico.

A spaciousness awaits
beyond the to-and-fro.

Behind the lofty gates,
a spaciousness awaits.
Past the loud debates,
farther than Yes or No,
a spaciousness awaits
beyond the to-and-fro.

Take the book of myth
with you into the wood
on your quest for truth.
Take the book of myth
which braids into one wreath
the living and the dead.
Take the book of myth
with you into the wood.

I don't know how to speak.
I or you or she?
Can people only talk
(I don't know how to speak)
perched on the rigid rock
of an identity?
I don't know how to speak:
I or you or she?

Surfaces confuse.
Down in the depths is law.
Investigate each face.
Surfaces confuse
with metamorphoses
of what you thought you saw.
Surfaces confuse.
Down in the depths is law.

What else can I bring?
I'm carrying my story,
this much-crumpled thing.
What else can I bring,
what humble offering
served as allegory?
What else can I bring?
I'm carrying my story.

Colors: red white gray.
Nouns: meadow forest gate.
It seems I must deploy
colors—red white gray—
to hold to clarity.
It's hard to get it right.
Colors: red white gray.
Nouns: meadow forest gate.

Safe as in a board game
moving from square to square
or in a stanza's room;
safe as in a board game,
a compact space to roam
and rules to tell me where.
Safe as in a board game
moving from square to square.

The waterfall descending
adores its destination.
I didn't say its ending.
The waterfall descending
in foam and sparkle, lending
dull rock its exultation . . .
The waterfall descending
adores its destination.

This one I want to hold
and that one give away,
now that I'm getting old.
This one I need to hold
until its tale is told
and it dries up for me.
This one I need to hold
and that one give away.

HURRY, RED FRUIT, DESCENT

November noon. I'm hurrying down Broadway.
Sharp sunlight.
Only two blocks from the subway,

and what's this? An enormous wooden crate
big enough to hold a small piano,
so wide pedestrians have to dodge around it,

as most do, deftly, barely slowing down
as they skirt this massive obstacle—
not a raised eyebrow, not a smile or frown,

as if ignoring made invisible
this great square box brimful of perfect bright
pomegranates—such a teetering pile

you'd think some would spill out onto the street
and roll away toward the realm of fable,
back where they came from. Rooted to the spot,

far from hurrying, I'm in a bubble.
Forgetting I'm supposed to catch a train,
I ponder fruit and this fruit's freight of trouble.

The pomegranates gleam in the thin sun,
and every one denotes a dark exchange:
a virgin picking flowers is carried down

out of sight, beyond her mother's range,
to the subway—the true underground
realm where things look shadowy and strange,

and where she, hungry, fails to understand
she must eat nothing, swallow not one seed
if she would return to her own land.

I think about the living and the dead
("I had not thought death had undone so many,"
Dante and then T. S. Eliot said)

numbly streaming down the street, like any
holiday shoppers—so many gifts to buy,
so little time, and time, we know, is money.

I think about the girl Persephone,
for whom somewhere a perfect red globe waits,
and about a larger symmetry.

For one abstracted moment it all fits—
the reciprocity, the master plan.
An unseen hand wielding a cleaver cuts

through tough skin and leathery membrane,
exposing seeds packed tidily inside.
For every single seed a destination!

Is each seed steered toward some allotted bride,
meted out neatly to the perfect daughter,
or does each girl select her seed instead?

Either way, they're made for one another.
Confronted by this dowry chest of red,
I feel the pressure of a fruitful future.

But now, emerging from my interlude
of reverie, I'm jostled by the flow
of traffic now collecting heft and speed

as people hurry where they want to go.
I join the crowd stampeding down the stairs
at Ninety-Sixth Street to the trains below

the season and the fruit, the sun and stars.

IN THE THEATER

No, I won't swallow the rest of the hemlock.
A single spoonful bitter on the tongue:
it hurts, it harms me, but here I still am,
deep in a red velvet orchestra seat
waiting for the curtain to rise on the premiere
of a lost Euripidean play.

Hemlock. Socrates? This tragedy
will not concern itself with the philosopher.
No extant tragedy does.
The title of this play is odd: *Success*.
The hemlock dregs still bitter in my mouth,
I settle back in my red seat to watch

myself clambering over jagged rocks.
A child is pointing toward the open sea.
"How could you get lost?" his wordless gesture
asks. How could I? There is only one way.
Sunlight shimmers over the wide gray water.
I shift in my red seat. The lights go down.

THREE

COVERED BASKET

A neighbor I don't recognize
hands me a basket covered with a napkin.
I lift a corner of the cloth, peek in:

one string of wooden beads,
one string of cowrie shells.
Komboloya. Prayer. Divination.

The basket is now mine
to carry for a while along a road
to where I do not know.

In the silence, pronouns change their shape.
Language washes its hands of daily chores.
Colors sharpen like so many knives.

Whenever it happens that my sight is scoured,
red hits me freshly:
bird, blossom, blood, and flame.

Years ago, carried down our long hall
and pointing to the fixture on the ceiling,
my son said his first word: *Ite! Ite!*

The flickering of what there are no words for,
or else too many, and all inexact.
I reach out to hold you.

I pull my arm back.
What are the names for what I feel for you,
for what I want from you,

for what I want to give you? Have to give you?
Are all these words the same?
A covered basket to pass on to the next reaching hand.

The color of the desert changes slowly
or swiftly (I don't know
by what cosmic criteria to judge)

as if the giant wing of some
creature unfathomably vast in flight
cast a moving shadow over the sweep of the land.

You have the power to change the pace and color.
You thumb the images on your iPad,
scrolling back and back to the beginning,

as we stand on Amsterdam Avenue
waiting for the light to change
on one of the longest nights of the year.

Dark of the moon, flickering flames, the first
menorah in my life in many years;
the first time I ever watched the candles

steadily from their lighting to their guttering.
Lambent epiphanies; eight aging sisters,
some burning with a brighter, more persistent

flame than others; dancers
agitated by an unseen breath.
Everyone sees visions.

I was late in learning to attend.
Mystery markers folded in a cloth,
the basket passes from hand to unseen hand,

its changing content hidden.
How little I know you.
At my age, at any age,

how does imagination
set about filling up the empty space
before and after? Narratives ramify

and dwindle in the distance. Red horizon.
Flickering candles. Dark of the moon. We walk
one last block together, say good night.

THE BREAK

The road was slick,
that much I knew.
I also knew
or think I knew
already who
but not quite why
and not yet how.
My feet gave way.
I slid on snow.
Put out my hand
to break the fall,
soften the blow
on the glassy track.
Above, blue sky.
Below, hard snow.
I lay on my back.
Was I okay?
No. Yes. No. Wait.
Something had broken.
I waited a bit,
then tried to test
my right wrist,
which looked and felt
wrong. No pain;
some other hurt
I cannot name.
Something had woken.
How to say it?
As if light
poured through a crack
not in dark night

but in life's ordinary day,
which was receding as I lay.
No blood, no cut,
but something new,
nameless, uncanny,
pouring through.
A wound? A breach?
A mortal crack?
What flowed in
and what leaked out?
Under the snow
a buried stream,
promise of heat
in wisps of steam.
How far below
was the opening?
How long had it been
in preparation,
the secret thaw,
the start of spring?
I caught my breath
and then I stood
up, took the bad wrist
in the good
hand, and walked back
a careful mile
on the slippery track.
January sun felt strong;
an icicle broke off and fell,
but the shadows were getting long.
In the ER an hour, two, three
(maybe the X-ray reminded me),
the dawn dream just before I woke
that day replayed: I'd been with you.
Side by side we were squeezing through
a gate. I remember it was white.

I remember the fit was tight.
We made it somehow—not quite whole,
as if we had to pay a toll
to the new country where together
we're still standing a year later,
each of us gazing at the other.

VALENTINE'S DAY

there was no time to be everything to each other
and so we fell back on a morph a melt
a translation into dancing letters
swimming forgetful bed and holey sheets
valentine red later I smelled your kisses
covering me consuming me and tasted
the silken skin the warm the stretch the smother
each one's assimilation of the other
and at the same time can I call it calm
symmetrical our mutual gaze exploring
faces bodies that can never fit
inside the eye too much and not enough
then in the park river trees birds renewal
snowmelt gleaming sun of afternoon
late late but no less source of coming spring
no time to be less than everything.

FULL AND EMPTY ROOM

Swan-shaped incense holder on the desk; your sweater
Hanging informally over the back of a chair;
Amulets in a catalog of kabbalah
Lying on the bookshelf, Lurianic.
Oil pastels, a pad of paper: throbbing
Menorah, dancing candles, drawn by you,

Glowing in the livid light of a February afternoon.
Oh absent and oh present,
Room full of silence, studio
Empty and full at once,
Which flavor shall I say prevails without you
Inside this hallowed space,
Tranquil as if caught inside a
Zen koan to which no one knows the answer?

BALANCING

To land in a story whose end I do not know—
as if we ever saw to any end—
I try to keep my balance, high and low.

The sliver of this moon, discreet and new—
waxing? Waning? I forget. They blend
in a sky whose limits we don't know.

Out of the silk and velvet bedroom now
to jagged crevices, uneven land
I stagger, lurching between high and low.

One foot. The other. Careful where I go.
Where am I going? I cannot pretend
to map this new terrain. Nor do I know

just what meanders led me here to you,
oasis or mirage. Beloved friend,
a shadow looms. Now something's swooping low,

a storm of wings exploding in the blue.
Light is pouring through a mortal wound.
I am afraid to see. I want to know.
I clutch at uprights, reeling, high and low.

CENTO

I didn't just dream you into being.
I drowned in the fire of having you, I burned
in the river of not having you, we lived
together for hours in a house of a thousand rooms
and we were parted for a thousand years.
I will need to be young until I'm old.
I have resolved to keep from looking back
to that ignorant age when the want
was unknown, when I could live without you.
Necessities I never knew I knew
until meeting you a few days
or many lifetimes ago—
but who am I to find a solution?
It's an impossibility to map the mind.
You can't remember
where it is you're supposed to be
or if there is even anywhere
other than here.
I need water and food and air
and someone who loves me never to leave.

We were running round and round the garden.
High walls: could joy escape?
A thick tree root bursting through a concrete square.
Could we get out? Did we want to?
We wanted to taste each other.
Mouths open each other up in their collision.
We recognized a flavor
that in those thousand years apart
we hadn't quite forgotten.

You change and change
and keep on changing
and none of it matters.
No time to be everything to each other,
no time to be less than everything.

Oh absent and oh present,
necessities I never knew I knew.
I have resolved to keep from looking back.

Set me as a seal upon thine heart,
as a seal upon thine arm:
for love is strong as death.
Two winds are blowing.
The death wind may be easier;
the gusts of love force people to make choices.
Here we stand at the crossroads.
Garden, red, and green and rich brown earth
from which what tree will grow?
I woke two months ago
to newly fallen snow.
It seemed we were about to cross a threshold.
I am not whole without you. See this crack?
How did I break it? Going through the gate.

Lines are included from poems by Sean Battle, Adam Bowser, Heather Katzoff,
Elizabeth Kim, Robert Pinsky, Ravi Shankar, Nathanael Tagg, Bryanna Tidmarsh,
and the Song of Songs.

AUBADE

Do not go to the danger of wish granted.
Do not fear the future. Rest
pillowed on joy, if joy will let me rest.

Hills and valleys of contiguous
bodies in morning light,
although that peach flush might be either sunrise
or sunset moving over
the mountains like a hand.

GREEN AND GOLD

Stivenson Magloire

Amidst the glossy dark-green foliage
of trees around the hotel pool,
I spy a low-hanging golden fruit.
So many trees whose names I do not know
and for the first time do not care to learn.
The overwhelming now in its countless inflections
cancels vocabulary: eyes lips skin
instead of words. Still in the pool,
floating on my back as the sun gets low,
I look at the mango, if that is what it is
(I think it is some wholly other fruit),
and suddenly smell garlic sautéed in butter.
Chefs in the kitchen under the trees
are getting the hors d'oeuvres ready.

Yesterday in a dim, airless gallery,
following your lead,
I hunted down an iconography
written in a grisly alphabet
yet full of life, the haunting gaze direct,
transcending Death. Death had in winning lost.
Art trumped death and life trumped art. Last night
(our third together—sleep
a whole new texture in a bed with you)
I gave you space and found myself at the border
of a far province in the king-sized bed,
a dimly lit hinterland where paintings ruled,
a region wholly devoted to the work
of the same painter, mysteriously killed,

stoned to death ("lapidated" was one word),
assassinated—why? A mystery
to be solved by iconography?
Death had won but also death had lost.

Garlic and butter. Glossy dark-green leaves.
Voices across the pool. A hanging fruit.
An azure splash. And as the sun goes down,
you sit by the window in our room,
drawing pictures of this this this time.
What to call it? Colors in your hands
trump words. Like the fruit,
like the solution to the mystery,
something I am at a loss to name.

THE LOST BOTTLE

Magnolia champaca

Given the sweet assignment
Write about this perfume,
I open the tiny vial
and dab some on my arm.
A meadow hot with blossoms—
tropical? Caribbean?
Something that smells of sun
and that embraces dark.
Jasmine? Magnolia? Plaka.
Taverna. Early seventies.
A copper pot of wine.
The Gypsy stops at our table
with her basket of white blossoms.
The one picked out for me—
I can smell it now.
An azure veil drapes
each expansive future
now desiccated, trapped
inside a flower's ghost,
which has the ghostly power
to bring what's vanished back.

Vanished: I lost the vial
or it lost itself.
Did I perhaps leave it
in the hotel in Haiti?
I thought I brought it home.
Wherever the container,
something did stow away,

invisible and weightless:
the genie memory,
recovering the promise
and pleasure of a night,
delivering the flushed
pounding heat of day.

ROOSEVELT HOSPITAL BLUES

I thought that nothing ever happened to me.
To other people, yes, but not to me.
But baby, I was wrong as I could be.

I slipped on the ice last January, broke my wrist.
Thinking about you, slipped and broke my wrist.
Forgot how long it was since I'd been kissed.

February, March—we grabbed what hours we could.
My wrist was in a cast but we grabbed what time we could.
It was never enough but it was always good.

April in Haiti: we visited some schools.
Went to Haiti, visited three high schools.
Back in a hotel, swam in a turquoise pool.

A tree grew by the pool, its fruit was gold.
A nameless tree, its fruit was glowing gold.
Let's live together until we're really old.

You sat in our room with your back to the setting sun.
You sat there haloed by the setting sun
Drawing a picture of me with nothing on.

My red bathing suit was drying on the bedspread.
We'd been making love all over the bed.
I want to live with you until we are dead.

They stoned this artist to death right in the street.
At thirty-one he died in a Pétionville street.
Well, death is cold but life is full of heat.

The eyes he painted stare from the other side.
Those eyes: a challenge from the other side.
They say: I'm dead but my spirit hasn't died.

You took your computer out of a little room.
Your magical visions migrated from that room.
Now our twin images wander in one home.

The lawyer in mascara looking like a raccoon,
The divorce lawyer disguised as a raccoon
Roots in a garbage pail under the moon.

You drew two snakes dancing on a bed of heat,
Pulsing lines in a radiant heart of heat.
We're not allowed to hold hands in the street.

Living with you is learning day by day,
Waking, sleeping, discoveries every day.
Pain in my belly won't get in the way.

Went to the doctor, didn't like what he said.
We held hands and listened to what the doctor said.
As long as I'm with you I'm not afraid.

He told me to go to Roosevelt Hospital ER,
Rush hour in the rain to the ER.
I hailed a rickshaw—next best thing to a car.

Riding in a rickshaw up Tenth Avenue,
Rickshaw pedaling up Tenth Avenue,
My CAT scan sucks but I'm in love with you.

Love is a rickshaw bumping along in the rain,
Our love is a ride over potholes in the rain.
It's too intense, don't ask me to explain.

We missed your birthday, when can we celebrate?
Now it's over maybe we can celebrate
As soon as the doc lets me eat red velvet cake.

We're on some journey sweet and fast and slow,
Some adventure moving fast then slow.
Let's go together, baby, wherever we go.

SAILING IN THE SKY

Doreen from Jamaica in the lounge with me
tells me her troubles and I tell her mine.
A long white cruise ship edges out to sea
down the strip of river we can spy
through buildings. Sunset's painting the horizon
blue, vermilion. Everything in view
is etched and glittering and crystalline.

This morning when they came to draw my blood
the sun was rising in a ball of flame.
Sunset, sunrise. We're sailing in the sky.
We're in an aerie here on the tenth floor.
Doreen says, "Paradise is at our feet."
The sliver of deep sky between two buildings
begins down on the street.

SYRUP AND A WAFFLE

Well, the sun came up like a big fried egg.
Over my horse I threw my leg.
Once my foot was in the stirrup
I drank my morning shot of syrup.

    Syrup and a waffle,
    syrup and a waffle,
    I took my rifle
    that I won at a raffle.

Time to ride around the range
on the lookout for anything strange.
I can arrest folks for a trifle.
Flying a tattered flag's unlawful.

    Syrup and a waffle,
    syrup and a waffle,
    when we're apart
    I miss you awful.

I ride around the dusty hills
righting wrongs and curing ills.
Love as sweet as maple syrup
keeps me going at a gallop.

I never thought that I would ride,
my trusty rifle by my side,
around the dusty frontier towns.
But life has many ups and downs.

Waffle and syrup,
waffle and syrup,
it may be cloudy
but it'll clear up.

From sunrise to sunset I roam,
when darkness falls I head for home,
home of the brave, land of the free,
where my baby waits for me.

Syrup and a waffle,
syrup and a waffle,
sit behind me
on the saddle.

Syrup and a waffle,
syrup and a waffle,
we're together
as we travel.

SUNROOF TEST-DRIVE ICE STORM

These monosyllables are versatile;
sun, test, ice double as adjectives.
As well as economical, they're magic,
like every feature of our fresh-linked lives:
matter-of-fact, enchanting, practical,
and love-struck all at once. Let me climb in
for a *test-drive*, intoxicating spin
in the graceful gray-green chariot
we'll agree to name, once we've bought her,
after the glaucous goddess, Zeus's daughter,
patron of wisdom, handicrafts, and war
(Athena is her name, Theenie for short),
whose help we'll need these next months, there's no doubt.
A divine patroness—what's that about?

Hybrid myth weds fable to prosaic
modes of protection. Look: apotropaic
blue beads dangling from the dash repel
jealousy, guilt, and every kind of spell
aimed at lovers by the Evil Eye
(lovers are natural targets, blind with joy).
Let's climb into our goddess, lock the door,
and drive through traffic: illness, patience, fear,
light and dark all dappled by desire.
Ice storm is her color's name. Let weather
change, she'll take us through the storm together,
through space and time to where we need to go.
From her *sunroof* I can see the sky.
I look up: azure. Then I turn to you.

AFTER INDEPENDENCE DAY

Love and illness and contingency:
this iridescent bubble triply blown
drifts and spins along an afternoon
of sluggish breezes. Fireworks lazily
pop in the distance. Not so distant. Boom.
From a small blue window of clear sky,
an arrow: lightning stabbing the horizon.

Thunder at the lake. So wait till night.
Study the iconography of fire:
flames in the dark that lick and leap. Desire
elusive when depended on, then there,
urgent, unlooked for: sudden summer heat.
Here's a hammock. Lie down and look up.
A green cathedral wavers in the air.

STILL LIVES

Tug of undertow deep into June.
The air is saturated, but no rain.
Trees filter sun out till late afternoon.

Rustling then roaring: is it wind
or the creek out of sight around a bend?
This climate feels familiar, damp and green.

Sometimes you want to sink into the ground,
sleep through the moody weather of the world.
It is as if our houses were set down,

however far apart, in one pantoum.
Thigh high, waist deep, lapping at a breast,
a structure marinating in its past . . .

Whose? The weight of years here: yours, not mine.
Yet who are you?
A congeries of changes. Me too.

Twin variations on in-between,
our houses rhyme,
each with its feathery lawn

sloping downhill, the gravity of time,
time which is slowing, choked with memories
rank as weeds. Who will chop them down?

Time which is sweeping all this out of sight,
brown stream into gray river into sea's
azure. Dear love, we do not stay the same.

Still life: you are dozing in the hammock,
each leaf, blade, petal, stem
glittering motionless at half past ten.

A day's clock. Your life and mine
compose a ballad with a green refrain
the houses are two stanzas in.

Clouds are drifting slowly right
to left, a Hebrew book. Now it's night.
No moon has risen yet, but there's moonlight.

TWO LAKES

It rained both days at the lake.
I stand at the crossroads here
buffeted by the changes
since the turn of the year
when we two began.
Each noun retains its name—
cloud, rock, lake,
morning, noon, night—
but nothing feels the same.
Everything is new.
Take the flow of time
since I have been with you.
The future turns a face
that's different back to me.
More unexpectedly,
so does my own past.
Those years I lived through
taste different to me now.
I kept on spinning out
threads of talk—to whom?
why?—and never paused.
Now I take a breath.
Now I fold in toward home.
Yes, the future's short.
Yes, the past is long.
The present, then? A nest
where we can be at rest?
It's not so simple, though.
Present is also past.
This afternoon at the lake
before the thunder came,

we climbed a gentle slope
and sat on a bank of green,
wildflowers all around.
It reminded me
of nineteen fifty-three:
a summer in Rangeley, Maine.
There was a sloping meadow
near the rented house by the lake
where I and my best friend
day after sunny day
played with our dolls each morning,
talking incessantly.
Some little girls do that.
Doll Rock, we named the spot.
Our fathers in the hot
city taught summer school;
the families rusticated
a month, but it seems more.
Missy and I were four.
I'd be five in November
and would start kindergarten
scarily soon, September.
The meadow. The sunlit rock.
The dolls. Our quiet talk.
How do you capture that?
What is the taste of safety?
What is the color of time?
Sixty years have gone.
Here at another lake
you and I climb a hill
and sit down on a rock.

ELEMENTAL: OFFERING TO YEMAYA

I waded into the water
and sprinkled salt on the waves
that splashed—toe, calf, knee, thigh—
and wetted my white skirt.
I prayed to my ocean mother,
who shifted pebbles under
my feet: *Come further in!*
And cleaned myself with coins
and offered a white lily
and offered a white rose.
One the foam swallowed up.
One the waves tossed back.
In one iteration
of your rendering,
the water was midnight-blue,
the white flower singed and black.
The sky was flame, then water
was on fire too.
Behind them, my old face:
a crone, attentive, rapt.
Where was the girl who walked
slowly into the sea,
her flounced white skirt hitched up?
Could both of them be me?
Whatever age I am,
O Mother, help me through.
Cleanse my weary belly.
I have life's work to do.

Drowned flower, white and black,
skeletal on the sand,

stripped to a husk by salt,
rinsed to the bone by foam,
the water gave you back.
What color was the water?
What color was the sky?
Ocean and sun and fire:
as my love mixed them up,
layered and played them back,
the piled-up icons sorted
themselves to elements
wordlessly crying out.

Drawn to the edge, to salt,
to pale-blue sucking foam
abruptly black as night,
I turned my back to the city
and walked to meet my mother.
Brook, river, lake, ah ocean,
I will meet you halfway,
as far as I can go,
and sprinkle you with salt
and chant my prayer to you.
O cleanse my weary belly.
O Mother, help me heal.
O Mother, steer me home.
I have love's work to do.

LYING IN WAIT

Lying in bed and waiting for the purple
bruises to fade from my arms,
I remember the grinding pebbles underfoot
when I gave in to the muscular embrace of the ocean.
Now I rest in the wash of what has been accomplished.
A shallow golden river is pouring itself over stones,
over this empty husk, scooped shell of waiting
for transformation. Also transportation:
I need a fresh itinerary now
a dismantled world is being reassembled;
new map of stars I gaze at from the cool
tank of silence where I lie back, bathe,
and wait for the purple to fade.

BLISS

Bliss was a dangerous diet at first. It went to my head
and then to my belly and settled in my gut.

As soon as the danger was given a date and a name,
the phantoms had to be pushed back into the shadows

so you and I could keep to the severe path of brightness
step by step. But once the danger receded

even a little, the phantoms reappeared
with renewed gusto. How could they not?

The grinding process, the daily and hourly
reentry into the welter of time, the deep-

worn grooves of years of unhappiness as habit
distracted us from the clarity of the world.

Elements, though, never disappear.
They shift. No, seasons shift. Here it is August.

Sun is glistening through the leaves and balls
of the sycamore tree I squint up into

as, two days out of the hospital,
I lie in your lap on the grass.

Water still flows from brook to river to ocean.
Tongues of fire still lick the black night sky.

Earth is still where we stand, sit, walk, lie.
One of these will receive us when we die.

Mortality, love blissfully conspire
to fan its flames, this perilous desire

to drain the cup of every precious sense
till we are folded back to elements.

But now I turn away from hot noon blue
to rest my eyes, my thoughts, my soul in you.

EQUIPOISE

Early light slants low across the lawn.
Cuplike, this little valley brims with sun.
Pages fill and empty. In the mist
of a still morning, nothing's out of reach.
Decades fade, the past glides into range,
recoverable, a pristine cobweb caught
motionless in one slat of morning light.
You're on your daily walk uphill and back.

Summer's end balances autumn's start.
One apple falls without a breath of wind,
but fruit past counting's hidden in the tall
wet grass. Like this valley now, my heart
is full. I start to climb the hill toward you.
My soul flies out to greet you coming down.

SLOW GREEN

The elements were stark: a winter wall,
snow, ice, snapped wrist. Through the break
I could just glimpse the color of the bone.
But cold and white, the January crust,
weren't the whole story. Seasons turn,
bones knit, a secret stirs beneath the snow.

I told myself
my cast, like winter, wouldn't last forever.
But there was no way to envision this
country of velvet silence on the far
side of a gate I had unlatched in sleep.
A nameless angel's finger to his lips:

unscaffolded by language, hold the thought?
Not thought, not word. Rather breath. A vow.
Sunlight this late August afternoon
tips its slow green syrup to the lawn.
Mercy so deep I never knew till now.
The break is mended. Here I am with you.

PARENTS

Form and content want to be each other,
wrote a poet now two decades dead.
Purpose beyond the play of light and color?
Nope, there is none, my beloved said.
He is a father and I am a mother,
he of a daughter, I a son, both grown.
But also now we nurture one another,

my joy, my heart, my self in you, my own
astonishing discovery, the mine
now yours, his, whose possession we forget.
Silent colors throbbing on a screen:
face to face lips and eyes, no words, give light
steering us past the arid paths we knew.
Each soul slides out of one and into two.

BUT IT'S TRUE

Mingled with all kinds of colors,
Sweetbitter unmanageable creature who steals in;
Oh liminal, oh only time will tell.
An azure implication: yes, it's true.
My soul slipped out of me to live in you.

River flowing underground
And on the eyes black sleep of night.
Turn of the kaleidoscope.
Rain falls into the river gray in blue,
Wet into wet, and I dissolve in you.

Through the hourglass. Down the rabbit hole.
Eros shook my mind like a mountain wind.
Thus is his cheek the map of days outworn.
Hypothesis improbable but true:
My soul bled out of me and into you.

Something has been postponed.
I burned in the river of not having you.
Low and straight I flew toward snowy mountains.
A paradox improbable but true:
My soul swooped out of me and into you.

My glass cannot persuade me I am old.
What I do is this; for this I came.
Three flags flap: joy, grief, change.
Salute them patriotically. True:
My soul waves like a flag when I see you.

The sun with its dumb-fuck optimism has risen again.
Lank grass, naked, shining after winter
When beauty lived and died as flowers do now.
A well of longing opened up, and through
Its star-reflecting waters I saw you.

We wanted to taste each other.
Stand and face me.
Green drapes the branches. Change.
Unshakable conviction that it's true:
My soul fell out of me and into you.

The clock holds its heartbeat for a moment.
I am broken with longing.
Had having and in quest to have, extreme:
Shake out the sheets. Old folds give way to new.
The bed's remade. I'm lying down with you.

DAFFODIL NOTEBOOK

A bunch of bright yellow daffodils
lies on the virgin pages of a notebook
whose paper is the color that used to be called eye-ease green—
either actually lies over the spread pages
or sprouts from them.

Daffodils: spring. So notebook: fall. Pages: leaves.
Goldengrove unleaving, Hopkins writes in "Spring and Fall."
But which spring, which fall no one is saying.
Any fall, all falls, all springs, any spring.

The daffodils are all blossoms and no stems
or else they are stem and blossom,
just as the notebook's lined pages are unwritten on
unless they bear some spidery faint scribbles.
Either or, both viable, both
preternaturally clear and possible.

If there were writing on the open pages,
the flowers would obscure it.
If someone were to shut the notebook,
it would crush the flowers.

Thank god then for Marlon's tutelary presence.
Marlon, your daughter's husband of four months,
is standing tall above, behind, or simply near the notebook,
helping it to stay open, holding the place,
using his index finger at once to mark the relevant passage
and to protect the integrity of the daffodils.

That there is a contrast, a dialogue,
even a fundamental dialectic
doesn't mean there has to be a conflict.
Marlon is Janus-faced, he looks at both
the past and future. So is the notebook; so
is any notebook Janus-faced:
it can be opened either way.
Spelling it backward, like a Hebrew book,
Till life became a legend of the dead,
Longfellow writes in "The Jewish Cemetery at Newport."
But these golden flowers will not permit
life to become a legend of the dead.
"A legend of the dead? Over our dead bodies,"
they say. "We are," they say, "a celebration of life."

My family, noses forever in books—they are the notebook.
Your family, juicier, more elemental,
the daffodils. Or both our long past lives,
much annotated, heavily scribbled over,
are the notebook, and our fresh new love
bursting from the green pages,
the daffodils. Bridal bouquet? And this:
the daffodils are the children we are too old to have
and the grandchildren we hope to have.

Daffodils, spring flowers, three dimensions
springing up from flatness. A strange gift,
but oh, a gift. *Accept the fucking compliment,*
you taught me to say, and I say it,
I say to all divinities over and over, *Thank you.*

Again. Notebook: past. Flowers: present, future.
Field of play, field of fecundity
springing from what compost of old pages?
Something startles me where I thought I was safest,
writes Whitman in "This Compost."

Again. It is awkward to write on pages overlaid by a bunch of flowers,
let alone pages from which flowers are growing.
The flower alphabet trumps the ABC of literature,
so all the pages, even if they were scribbled over,
cleanse themselves. The book of life stays open
and accommodates flowers. Close it, you crush the flowers
and the golden gift is bruised,
battered, diminished, lost.

I desire both notebook and daffodils.
I can have both. In fact I must have both.
Here they both are.
I desire both daffodils and notebook,
and life tells me to embrace what is perishable
rather than choosing the record of what was.

Homer says prophets know what was, what is, what will be.
And so do dreams. Homer says,
As the generations of leaves, so are the generations of men.
Or as the generations of daffodils.
Homer is the contents of the notebook.
And Homer is the flower, but undying.
It is notebooks that suffer damage from hurricanes and time
but there is a living word that sprouts again.
It is daffodils that bloom afresh each spring.
We commit our love of daffodils to notebooks
if we cannot help it. I love you.
As I write this in my notebook,
joyful sprouting pushes the pages open.

POETREEF

for SG with love and with gratitude to GS

Rainwater pouring down through cedar shingles,
ocean water washing in over the veranda:
what storms have battered this house for years I can only imagine,
as I can only imagine the parties that must have taken place here,
smells of cooking, marijuana smoke,
echoes of laughter lingering in the heavy air.

A row of books leans higgledy-piggledy along the kitchen counter,
mildewy, mottled, pages stuck or loose.
Who chose and brought each one to this island?
Whose hands touched them? What
mix of expectations, wants and needs,
impulses, choices, loans, contingencies
contributed to this macédoine of paper?
Hurricanes: waters rose and pages floated.
I'll drown my book, said the magician
as he left another island. Later
some books had to be discarded.
Others were left open
so their pages could dry in the sun.

I pick up a mold-mottled copy of *Murder in the Cathedral*.
Faintly familiar, the words on the page
stay urgent, clear, foreboding.
There are books in the house, our generous host's instructions advise,
but are they the books you want to read?
It depends on what you mean by reading.
Here I browse, I pounce, I skip, I skim, pick and choose.
I put a finger blindly in the book
and open it there. *Sortes Vergilianae.*

what wrong
Shall the bird's song cover, the green tree cover, what wrong
Shall the fresh earth cover? We wait, and the time is short
But waiting is long.
I take another book and open it: *Come,*
Leave the agate
Hard smoke, O speed that kills;
On your diamond skates, scratch
The mirror of the sick.
The walls
The walls
Have ears
And mirrors
Eyes of a lover.
Cocteau. The inscription on the title page
of *Mid-Century French Poets* (1955)
is blurred and blotched red ink, illegible.
Probably decades old, it resembles
fresh blood diluted with seawater.
The two sections of the introduction
are titled "The Legacy of Symbolism"
and "The Generations."
Legacy. Generations.
Mirrors. Eyes of a lover.
Who has loved in this house?
Who has looked in the mirror?
Who has kept the front door open,
as I am doing now,
to write at the long table
in the morning sun?
The mist and damage of hurricanes past and future,
the smoke of countless bonfires, salt marks of countless lives,
the touch of vanished hands.
Who has done his day's work?
(This from a crack-spined Modern Library Whitman)

Who will soonest be through with his supper?
Who wishes to walk with me?

I look down at my hands:
brown age spots well along.
At my belly scarred from last summer's surgery.
None of this matters, it is only the weather of mortality.
We are alive. Our days and nights are lit
and lifted by the love that floated us to this island.

Love when the roosters crow in the early morning
when the sky is turning from white to blue;
at noon in the big dim russet bedroom,
slats of sun slanting through cedar louvers,
Anansi alert on the white plaster wall;
at night when the moon shines down on the coral reefs
and etches shadows black.

It takes twenty-four hours to feel at home in a house,
to make peace with its ghosts,
to open its battered books and find your place.
There are past lives in the house,
but are they the lives you want to have lived,
the friends you want to have made?
Do we have a choice?
You are the friend I have made for the rest of my life.
You are my love for as long as the two of us have.
For years my life demanded so little of me.
The books I read and taught were not storm-salted,
but worn nevertheless. They were books I knew already.
I filled my days, I talked and talked over the abyss,
but there was nothing new to learn to love.
Now here I am on an island in warm seas
in the middle of winter, and on the island

is a house brimful of past lives
and mildewed stories and present love, a house
I have been waiting to visit all my life.
Here we are together.
You unlocked the gates and the house let us in.